C000178635

STAYING A HEAD
The Stress Management Secrets of Successful School-Leaders
Pocket Handbook

Viv Grant

Illustrations: Sye Watts

Staying A Head
The Stress Management Secrets of Successful School Leaders
Pocket Handbook

First published in 2014 by
Integrity Coaching
4 Abercrombie Street,
London, SW11 2JD
www.integritycoaching.co.uk

Illustrations: Sye Watts
www.syewatts.co.uk

Cover design and typeset by EPLS Design
www.eplsdesign.com

This book is printed on demand so no copies will be remaindered or pulped.

ISBN 978-0-9929250-2-4

The right of Viv Grant to be identified as the author of this work has been asserted in accordance with sections 77 and 78 of the Copyright design and Patents Act 1988.

A CIP catalogue record for this book is available from the British Library.

All rights reserved. No part of this work maybe reproduced in any material form (including photocopying or storing in any medium by electronic means and whether or not transiently or incidentally to some other use of this publication) without the written permission of the copyright holder except in accordance with the provisions of the Copyright, Designs and Patents Act 1988. Applications for the copyright holder's written permission to reproduce any part of this publication should be addressed to the publishers.

Copyright 2014 Viv Grant

This pocket book is dedicated to school leaders everywhere. Every day, they overcome the obstacles inherent in their role, harness their passion and commitment, and continue to make a real and long lasting difference to the children in our schools. Thank you!

INTRODUCTION

In an article written for the New York Times in 2012, Bill Gates said,

"Developing a systematic way to help teachers get better is the most powerful idea in education today. The surest way to weaken it is to twist it into a capricious exercise in public shaming. Let's focus on creating a personnel system that truly helps teachers to improve."

This pocket handbook seeks to illustrate the current educational environment and its impact on school leaders.

It also seeks to provide an overview of the type of 'personnel' activities that school leaders need to engage in, if they are to overcome the stresses of school leadership and maintain their ability to lead and inspire others.

The stress that you experience
as a school leader may
mean that...

Sometimes confidence fails you and the inner bridge that you have to cross to get to work can become weak and unsteady.

In order to maintain an 'outstanding' performance you have to keep your fears and self doubt hidden from others.

As you try to sort out both your own and everyone else's problems your head can sometimes feel like a plate full of spaghetti!

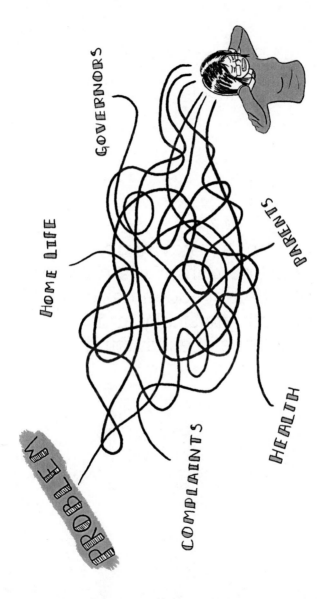

Continually having to perform in front of a number of different audiences can be both physically and emotionally exhausting.

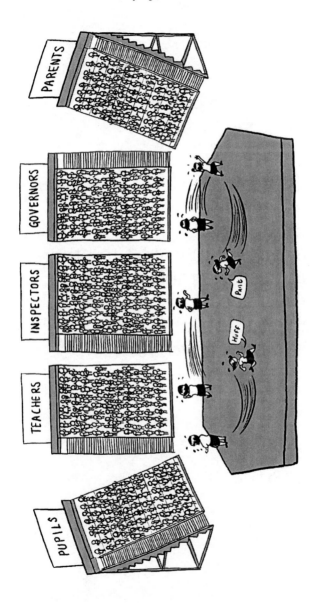

You constantly give to others and seek to meet everyone else's needs, without ever being able to stop long enough to give back to yourself.

THE SACRIFICE SYNDROME

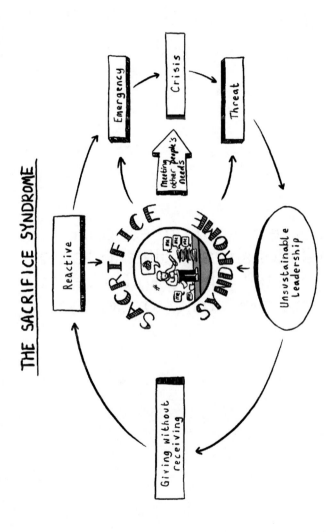

Some of your professional relationships do little to bolster your self esteem and belief in your own ability to succeed.

As a result, come the end of the day, when you take off your 'super hero' cloak, the stresses and strains of your role can feel all too much!

19

To overcome the stresses
of school leadership and...

...help maintain your ability
to lead and inspire others...

Start by being kind to yourself and understanding that no matter how well concealed it might be, every school leader's journey begins at the point of unconscious incompetence; it is only with time, patience and understanding and an environment that facilitates personal growth, that a school leader can reach the point of unconscious competence.

MASLOW'S FOUR STAGES OF LEARNING MODEL

Unconscious Incompetence
You don't know that you don't know how to do something

Conscious Incompetence
You know that you don't know how to do something and it bothers you

Conscious Competence
You know that you know how to do something and it takes effort

Unconscious Competence
You know how to do something and it is second nature.

Find a space that allows you to develop greater self-awareness and understanding about who you are as a leader.

THE JOHARI WINDOW

Talk to someone who believes in you and will help you come to your own solutions.

Make time to be still and set your thoughts free.

Build professional relationships
that are built on mutual trust
and respect.

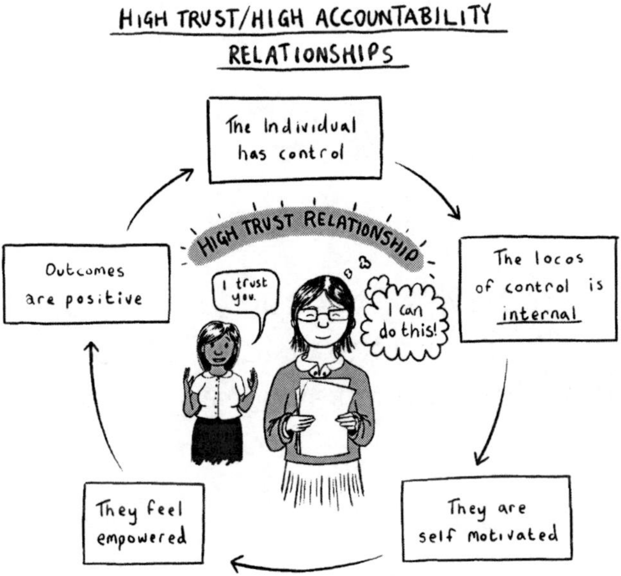
HIGH TRUST/HIGH ACCOUNTABILITY RELATIONSHIPS
The Individual has control
The locos of control is internal
They are self motivated
They feel empowered
Outcomes are positive
HIGH TRUST RELATIONSHIP
I trust you.
I can do this!

Learn how to stay true to who you really are and the vision that you have for yourself and your school.

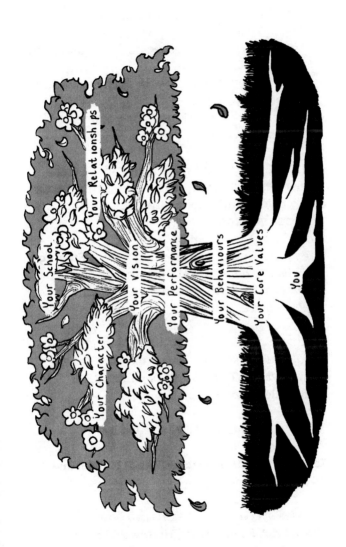

If you are a school leader struggling with:

- The pressures of increased public scrutiny and accountability
- The effect stress has on your ability to lead and perform at your best
- The impact stress is having on your personal life and overall well-being

and would like to find ways to rise above these challenges, so that you are able to maintain your ability to lead and inspire others, then along with this book you can:

- Buy the Kindle or paper back copy of **Staying a Head: The Stress Management Secrets of Successful School Leaders**. The book has been described as:

"A fantastic read – certainly something all senior and middle leaders should have on their book shelves."
Andrew Parkin, Principal, St Dominic's Sixth Form College, London

"Wise, timely and very well needed by the profession."
Kathryn Pugh, Head teacher, The St Marylebone CE School, London

"A series of coaching sessions in a book! Perfect."
Alison Kriel, Head teacher, Northwold Primary School, London

- Visit **www.integritycoaching.co.uk** and,
  - Sign up for our "Staying A Head" Newsletter
  - Browse our website and find out more about the coaching services that we provide for school leaders
  - Arrange an initial one to one meeting focused on meeting your needs as a school leader

NOTES:

Lightning Source UK Ltd.
Milton Keynes UK
UKOW04f0839231014

240534UK00007B/99/P